All Men Seek God

ALL MEN
SEEK GOD

The Quest for Faith

in the Words of Great

Leaders and Thinkers

Selected by

Dean Walley

With Illustrations by

Ronald M. LeHew

♔

Hallmark Editions

CONTENTS

The Quest for Faith, 5

Faith, Hope, and Love, 21

By Prayer Set Free, 33

One God for All Men, 41

The Hope of Immortality, 53

THE QUEST FOR FAITH

The Fundamental Emotion

The most beautiful experience we can have is the mysterious. It is the fundamental emotion which stands at the cradle of true art and true science. A knowledge of the existence of something we cannot penetrate, our perceptions of the profoundest reason and the most radiant beauty, which only in their most primitive forms are accessible to our minds—it is this knowledge and this emotion that constitute true religiosity; in this sense, and in this alone, I am a deeply religious man.

ALBERT EINSTEIN

A Genuine Faith

A genuine faith must recognize the fact that it is through a dark glass that we see; though by faith we do penetrate sufficiently to the heart of the mystery not to be overwhelmed by it. A genuine faith resolves the mystery of life by the mystery of God. It recognizes that no aspect of life or existence explains itself, even after all known causes and consequences have been traced. All known existence points beyond itself. To realize that it points beyond itself to God is to assert that the mystery of life does not dissolve life into meaninglessness. Faith in God is faith in some ultimate unity of life, in some final comprehensive purpose which holds all the various, and frequently contradictory, realms of coherence and meaning together. REINHOLD NIEBUHR

The Search for God

God is still in his universe. Our new technological and scientific developments can neither banish him from the microscopic compass of the atom nor from the vast, unfathomable ranges of interstellar space. Living in a universe in which the distances of some heavenly bodies must be dated in terms of billions of light years, modern man exclaims with the Psalmist of old, "When I consider thy heavens, the work of thy fingers, the moon and the stars, which thou hast ordained; what is man, that thou art mindful of him? and the son of man, that thou visitest him?"

I would urge you to give priority to the search for God. Allow his spirit to permeate your being. To meet the difficulties and challenges of life you will need him. Before the ship of your life reaches its last harbor, there will be long, drawn-out storms, howling and jostling winds, and tempestuous seas that make the heart stand still. If you do not have a deep and patient faith in God, you will be powerless to face the delays, disappointments, and vicissitudes that inevitably come. Without God, all of our efforts turn to ashes and our sunrises into darkest nights. Without him, life is a meaningless drama in which the decisive scenes are missing. But with him, we are able to rise from tension-packed valleys to the sublime heights of inner peace, and find radiant stars of hope against the nocturnal bosom of life's most depressing nights. St. Augustine was right: "Thou hast created us for thyself, and our heart cannot be quieted till it find repose in thee." MARTIN LUTHER KING, JR.

Steady Radiance

God does not die on the day when we cease to believe in a personal deity, but we die on the day when our lives cease to be illumined by the steady radiance, renewed daily, of a wonder, the source of which is beyond all reason.

DAG HAMMARSKJOLD

Tarry To Enjoy

Great is the blindness and exceeding the folly of many souls that are ever seeking God, continuously sighing after God, and frequently desiring God: whilst, all the time, they are themselves the tabernacles of the living God . . . since their soul is the seat of God, in which He continuously reposes. Now who but a fool deliberately seeks a tool which he possesses under lock and key? or who can use and profit by an instrument which he is seeking? or who can draw comfort from food for which he hungers, but which he does not relish at leisure? Like unto all this is the life of many a just soul, which ever seeks God and never tarries to enjoy Him; and all the works of such an one are, on this account, less perfect.

st. THOMAS AQUINAS

A Religious Outlook

During the past thirty years, people from all the civilized countries of the earth have consulted me. Many hundreds of patients have passed through my hands . . . . Among all my patients in the second half of life—that is to say, over thirty-five—there has not been one whose problem in the last resort was not that of finding a religious outlook on life. It is safe to say that every one of them fell ill because he had lost what the living religions of every age have given to their followers, and none of them has been really healed who did not regain his religious outlook.   CARL JUNG

A Cosmos, Not a Chaos

I paused to listen to the silence. My breath, crystallized as it passed my cheeks, drifted on a breeze gentler than a whisper. The wind vane pointed toward the South Pole. Presently the wind cups ceased their gentle turning as the cold killed the breeze. My frozen breath hung like a cloud overhead.

The day was dying, the night was being born —but with great peace. Here were the imponderable processes and forces of the cosmos, harmonious and soundless. Harmony, that was it! That was what came out of the silence —a gentle rhythm, the strain of a perfect chord, the music of the spheres, perhaps.

It was enough to catch that rhythm, momentarily to be myself a part of it. In that instant I could feel no doubt of man's oneness with the universe. The conviction came that that

rhythm was too orderly, too harmonious, too
perfect to be a product of blind chance—that,
therefore, there must be purpose in the whole
and that man was part of that whole and not
an accidental offshoot. It was a feeling that
transcended reason; that went to the heart of
man's despair and found it groundless. The
universe was a cosmos, not a chaos; man was
as rightfully a part of that cosmos as were the
day and night.

ADMIRAL RICHARD E. BYRD

The World Is Beautiful

We lead a difficult life, not always managing
to fit our actions to the vision we have of the
world. (And when I think I have caught a
glimpse of the color of my fate, it shoots off
out of sight.) We struggle and suffer to recon-
quer our solitude. But a day comes when the
earth has its simple and primitive smile. Then,
it is as if the struggles and life within us were
rubbed out. Millions of eyes have looked at
this landscape, and for me it is like the first
smile of the world. It takes me out of myself, in
the deepest meaning of the expression. It as-
sures me that nothing matters except my love,
and that even this love has no value for me

unless it remains innocent and free. It denies me a personality, and deprives my suffering of its echo. The world is beautiful, and this is everything. The great truth which it patiently teaches me is that neither the mind nor even the heart has any importance. And that the stone warmed by the sun or the cypress tree swelling against the empty sky set a boundary to the only world in which "to be right" has any meaning: nature without men. This world reduces me to nothing. It carries me to the very end. Without anger, it denies that I exist. And, agreeing to my defeat, I move toward a wisdom where everything has been already conquered—except that tears come into my eyes, and this great sob of poetry makes me forget the truth of the world.

ALBERT CAMUS

Open To Light

I call that mind free which jealously guards its intellectual rights and powers, which calls no man master, which does not content itself with a passive or hereditary faith, which opens itself to light whencesoever it may come, which receives new truth as an angel from Heaven.   WILLIAM ELLERY CHANNING

Something of God

I hear and behold God in every object, yet
understand God not in the least,
Nor do I understand who there can be more
wonderful than myself.
Why should I wish to see God better than
this day?
I see something of God each hour of the
twenty-four, and each moment then,
In the faces of men and women I see God, and
in my own face in the glass,
I find letters from God dropped in the street,
and every one is signed by God's name,
And I leave them where they are, for I know
that wheresoe'er I go
Others will punctually come forever and ever.

WALT WHITMAN

'A Great Thought'

To-day there is a wide measure of agreement,
which on the physical side of science ap-
proaches almost to unanimity, that the stream
of knowledge is heading towards a non-me-
chanical reality; the universe begins to look
more like a great thought than like a great ma-
chine. Mind no longer appears as an accidental

intruder into the realm of matter; we are beginning to suspect that we ought rather to hail it as the creator and governor of the realm of matter—not of course our individual minds, but the mind in which the atoms out of which our individual minds have grown exist as thoughts.

The new knowledge compels us to revise our hasty first impressions that we had stumbled into a universe which either did not concern itself with life or was actively hostile to life. The old dualism of mind and matter, which was mainly responsible for the supposed hostility, seems likely to disappear, not through matter becoming in any way more shadowy or insubstantial than heretofore, or through mind becoming resolved into a function of the working of matter, but through substantial matter resolving itself into a creation and manifestation of mind. We discover that the universe shows evidence of a designing or controlling power that has something in common with our own individual minds—not, so far as we have discovered, emotion, morality, or aesthetic appreciation, but the tendency to think in the way which, for want of a better word, we describe as mathematical. And while much in it may be hostile to the material appendages of life, much also is akin to the fundamental activities of life; we are not so much strangers or intruders in the universe as we first thought. Those inert atoms in the primaeval slime which first began to foreshadow the attributes of life were putting themselves more, and not less, in accord with the fundamental nature of the universe.   SIR JAMES JEANS

The Need for God

When a man surveys his past from middle age he must surely ask himself what those bygone years have taught him. If I have learned anything in the swift unrolling of the web of time . . . it is the virtue of tolerance, of moderation in thought and deed, of forbearance toward one's fellowmen.

I have come also to acknowledge the great illusion which lies in the pursuit of a purely material goal. What slight satisfaction lies in temporal honour and worldly grandeur . . . ! All the material possessions for which I strove so strenuously mean less to me now than a glance of love from those who are dear to me.

Above all am I convinced of the need, irrevocable and inescapable, of every human heart, for God. No matter how we try to escape, to lose ourselves in restless seeking, we cannot separate ourselves from our divine source. There is no substitute for God.

A. J. CRONIN

An Ordinary Man

I saw myself, in dream, a youth, almost a boy, in a low-pitched wooden church. The slim wax candles gleamed, spots of red, before the old pictures of the saints.

A ring of colored light encircled each tiny flame. Dark and dim it was in the church . . . . But there stood before me many people. All fair-haired, peasant heads. From time to time they began swaying, falling, rising again, like the ripe ears of wheat, when the wind of summer passes in low undulation over them.

All at once some man came up from behind and stood beside me.

I did not turn towards him; but at once I felt that this man was Christ.

Emotion, curiosity, awe overmastered me suddenly. I made an effort . . . and looked at my neighbour.

A face like every one's, a face like all men's faces. The eyes looked a little upwards, quietly and intently. The lips closed, but not compressed; the upper lip, as it were, resting on the lower; a small beard parted in two. The hands folded and still. And the clothes on him like everyone's.

"What sort of Christ is this" I thought. "Such an ordinary, ordinary man! It can't be!"

I turned away. But I had hardly turned my eyes away from this ordinary man when I felt again that it really was none other than Christ standing beside me.

Again I made an effort over myself . . . . And again the same face, like all men's faces, the same everyday though unknown features.

And suddenly my heart sank, and I came to myself. Only then I realized that just such a face—a face like all men's faces—is the face of Christ.   IVAN TURGENEV

Not by Bread Alone

The real problem that confronts us, and it is a great problem, is how to adjust religion to science, faith to knowledge, ideality to reality, for adjustment in the reverse direction will never happen. Facts cannot be eliminated by ideals and it is too late in the history of the world to attempt to refute the findings of science by sentimental objections or supposed theological difficulties. If science makes mistakes, science must furnish the cure; it can never be done by church councils, state legislatures, nor even by popular vote.

The only possible remedy for the present deplorable condition is not less but more and better science and education; science that recognizes that the search for truth is not the whole of life, that both scientific reality and religious ideality are necessary to normal, happy, useful living. We must keep our feet on the ground of fact and science, but lift our heads into the atmosphere of ideals. "To the solid ground of Nature trusts the mind that builds for aye." Education from the earliest years must teach love rather than hate, human brotherhood rather than war, service rather than selfishness; it must develop good habits of body and mind; it must instil reverence, not only for truth but also for beauty and righteousness.

"Where there is no vision, the people perish." Man cannot live by bread alone; he must have ideals and aspirations, faith and hope and love. In short, he must have a religion. The world never needed a religion of high ideals and aspirations more than it needs it now. But the old religion of literalism and of slavish regard to the authority of church or book, while well suited to some minds, cannot serve the needs of those who have breathed the air of science . . . .

The greatest exponents of evolution, such as Darwin, Huxley, Asa Gray, and Weismann, have maintained that there is evidence of some governance and plan in Nautre. This is the fundamental article of all religious faith. If there is no purpose in the universe, or in evolution, or in man, then indeed there is no God and no good. But if there is purpose in nature and in human life, it is only the imperfection of our mental vision that leads us sometimes to cry in despair: "Vanitas vanitatum, all is vanity." No one can furnish scientific proof of the existence or nature of God, but atheism leads to pessimism and despair, while theism leads to faith and hope. "By their fruits ye shall know them."   EDWIN GRANT CONKLIN

As rivers have their source in some far-off fountain, so the human spirit has its source. To find this fountain of spirit is to learn the secret of heaven and earth.   LAO-TSE

FAITH, HOPE AND LOVE

Mysteries of the Kingdom

The same day went Jesus out of the house, and sat by the sea side.

And great multitudes were gathered together unto him, so that he went into a ship, and sat; and the whole multitude stood on the shore.

And he spake many things unto them in parables, saying, Behold, a sower went forth to sow;

And when he sowed, some seeds fell by the way side, and the fowls came and devoured them up:

Some fell upon stony places, where they had not much earth: and forthwith they sprung up, because they had no deepness of earth:

And when the sun was up, they were scorched; and because they had no root, they withered away.

And some fell among thorns; and the thorns sprung up, and choked them:

But others fell into good ground, and brought forth fruit, some an hundredfold, some sixty-fold, some thirtyfold. . . .

Another parable put he forth unto them,

saying, The kingdom of heaven is like to a grain of mustard seed, which a man took, and sowed in his field:

Which indeed is the least of all seeds: but when it is grown, it is the greatest among herbs, and becometh a tree, so that the birds of the air come and lodge in the branches thereof.

Another parable spake he unto them; The kingdom of heaven is like unto leaven, which a woman took, and hid in three measures of meal, till the whole was leavened . . . .

Again, the kingdom of heaven is like unto treasure hid in a field; the which when a man hath found, he hideth, and for joy thereof goeth and selleth all that he hath, and buyeth that field.

Again, the kingdom of heaven is like unto a merchant man, seeking goodly pearls:

Who, when he had found one pearl of great price, went and sold all that he had, and bought it.

Again, the kingdom of heaven is like unto a net, that was cast into the sea, and gathered of every kind:

Which, when it was full, they drew to shore, and sat down, and gathered the good into vessels, but cast the bad away.

MATTHEW 13: 1-8, 31-33, 44-48

Compassion for Them

The wise, full of love, worship me, believing that I am the origin of all, and that all moves on through me. Placing their minds on me, offering their lives to me, instructing each other, and speaking about me, they live always contented and happy. To these, who are constantly devoted, and who worship with love, I give that knowledge by which they attain to me. And remaining in their hearts, I destroy, with the brilliant lamp of knowledge, the darkness born of ignorance in such men only, out of compassion for them.   THE BHAGAVADGITA

Love All

Love all God's creation, both the whole and every grain of sand. Love every leaf, every ray of light. Love the animals, love the plants, love each separate thing. If thou love each thing thou wilt perceive the mystery of God in all; and when once thou perceive this, thou wilt thenceforward grow every day to a fuller understanding of it: until thou come at last to love the whole world with a love that will then be all-embracing and universal.

FYODOR DOSTOEVSKI

I Never Saw a Moor

I never saw a Moor—
I never saw the Sea—
Yet know I how the Heather looks
And what a Billow be.

I never spoke with God
Nor visited in Heaven—
Yet certain am I of the spot
As if the Checks were given—

EMILY DICKINSON

To Grow in Love

I believe in God, who is for me spirit, love, the principle of all things. I believe that God is in me, as I am in Him. I believe that the true welfare of man consists in fulfilling the will of God. I believe that from the fulfillment of the will of God there can follow nothing but that which is good for me and for all men. I believe that the will of God is that every man should love his fellow-men, and should act toward others as he desires that they should act toward him. I believe that the reason of life is for each of us simply to grow in love. I believe that this growth in love will contribute more

24

than any other force to establish the Kingdom of God on earth. To replace a social life in which division, falsehood and violence are all-powerful with a new order in which humanity, truth and brotherhood will reign.

LEO TOLSTOY

At the Edge of Mystery

There has always been more to know than one man could know; there have always been modes of feeling that could not move the same heart; there have always been deeply held beliefs that could not be composed into a synthetic union. Yet never before today has the diversity, the complexity, the richness so clearly defied hierarchical order and simplification, never before have we had to understand the complementary, mutually not compatible ways of life and recognize choice between them as the only course of freedom. Never before today has the integrity of the intimate, the detailed, the true art, the integrity of craftsmanship and the preservation of the familiar, of the humorous and the beautiful stood in more massive contrast to the vastness of life, the greatness of the globe, the otherness of people, the otherness of ways, and the all-encompassing dark.

This is a world in which each of us, knowing his limitations, knowing the evils of superficiality and the terrors of fatigue, will have to cling to what is close to him, to what he knows, to what he can do, to his friends and his tradition and his love, lest he be dissolved in a universal confusion and know nothing and love nothing. It is at the same time a world in which none of us can find hieratic prescription or general sanction for any ignorance, any insensitivity, any indifference. When a friend tells us of a new discovery we may not understand, we may not be able to listen without jeopardizing the work that is ours and closer to us; but we cannot find in a book or canon—and we should not seek—grounds for hallowing our ignorance. If a man tells us that he sees differently than we or that he finds beautiful what we find ugly, we may have to leave the room, from fatigue or trouble; but that is our weakness and our default. If we must live with a perpetual sense that the world and the men in it are greater than we and too much for us, let it be the measure of our virtue that we know this and seek no comfort. Above all let us not proclaim that the limits of our powers correspond to some special wisdom in our choice of life, of learning, or of beauty.

This balance, this perpetual, precarious, impossible balance between the infinitely open and the intimate, this time—our twentieth century—has been long in coming; but it has come. It is, I think, for us and our children, our only way. . . .

This cannot be an easy life. We shall have a rugged time of it to keep our minds open and to keep them deep, to keep our sense of beauty and our ability to make it, and our occasional ability to see it in places remote and strange and unfamiliar; we shall have a rugged time of it, all of us, in keeping these gardens in our villages, in keeping open the manifold, intricate, casual paths, to keep these flourishing in a great, open, windy world; but this, as I see it, is the condition of man; and in this condition we can help, because we can love, one another.

J. ROBERT OPPENHEIMER

The Right Path

People who have a religion should be glad, for not everyone has the gift of believing in heavenly things. You don't necessarily even have to be afraid of punishment after death; hell and heaven are things that a lot of people can't accept; but still a religion, it doesn't matter which, keeps a person on the right path. It isn't the fear of God but the upholding of one's own honor and conscience.   ANNE FRANK

Man's Work

What else can I do, a lame old man, but sing hymns to God? If I were a nightingale, I would do the nightingale's part; if I were a swan, I would do as a swan. But now I am a rational creature, and I ought to praise God: this is my work; I do it, nor will I desert my post, so long as I am allowed to keep it. And I exhort you to join me in this same song.   EPICTETUS

God's Perfection

But what is it that I love when I love You? Not the beauty of any bodily thing, nor the order of seasons, not the brightness of light that re-joices the eye, nor the sweet melodies of all songs, nor the sweet fragrance of flowers and ointments and spices: not manna or honey, not the limbs that carnal love embraces. None of these things do I love in loving my God. Yet in a sense I do love light and melody and fra-grance and food and embrace when I love my God—the light and the voice and the fragrance and the food and embrace in the soul, when that shines upon my soul which no place can contain, that voice sounds which no tongue can take from me, I breathe that fragrance which no wind scatters, I eat the food which is not lessened by eating, and I lie in the embrace which satiety never comes to sunder. That it is that I love, when I love my God.

ST. AUGUSTINE

A Rainbow Trail

Walk on a rainbow trail; walk on a trail of song, and all about you will be beauty. There is a way out of every dark mist, over a rainbow trail. NAVAJO SONG

A Unique Soul

I was crossing a little stream near Inchy Wood and actually in the middle of a stride from bank to bank, when an emotion never experienced before swept down upon me. I said, "That is what the devout Christian feels, that is how he surrenders, his will to the will of God." I felt an extreme surprise, for my whole imagination was pre-occupied with the pagan mythology of ancient Ireland. I was marking in red ink, upon a large map, every sacred mountain. The next morning I awoke near dawn, to hear a voice saying, "The love of God is infinite for every human soul because every human soul is unique, no other can satisfy the same need in God."

WILLIAM BUTLER YEATS

A Healthy Instinct

This is the stupendous fact about man and his spiritual striving after God. It is not faith; it is not a contradiction of reason; it is merely a healthy instinct. It is man's total response to the universe through his moral nature. It is not the antithesis of reason; it is the higher reason.

LIN YUTANG

BY PRAYER SET FREE

As We Worship

That God has related Himself to us is not proven; but it is not implausible to expect that He has, does, and will. The experience of the people of God, of the old and new Israel, of the people of the Bible and of the Church, is that God has dealt with us, does deal with us and will continue to deal with us. This he does, of course, in manifold ways, but especially when we grow quiet, shut out the clamor of the world and the claims of the idols. Especially does He do this as we worship. Our adoration, our contrition, our prayers, and our acts of thanksgiving do not fall on deaf ears. These are not merely psychological exercises— though they are this; they are met on the other side by God's action. When we raise our hand to take God's hand, He does take our hand.

JAMES A. PIKE

It is not necessary to know something about God in order really to believe in Him: many true believers know how to talk to God but not about Him. MARTIN BUBER

On Prayer

A hasty kind of reasoning may hold that praying is an unprofitable act, because a man's prayer does not really change the Unchangeable; but even if this in the process of time were desired, might not changeable man come easily to regret that he had changed God? The true kind of reasoning is therefore the only desirable kind as well; prayer does not change God, but changes him who prays.

SOREN KIERKEGAARD

By Prayer Set Free

If we take the word "prayer" in the wider sense as meaning every kind of inward communion or conversation with the power recognized as divine, we can easily see that scientific criticism leaves it untouched . . . . The religious phenomenon, studied as an inner fact, and apart from ecclesiastical or theological complications, has shown itself to consist everywhere, and at all its stages, in the consciousness which individuals have of an intercourse between themselves and higher powers with which they feel themselves to be related . . . . Through prayer, religion insists, things which cannot be realized in any other manner come about: energy which but for prayer would be bound is by prayer set free and operates in some part, be it objective or subjective, of the world of facts. WILLIAM JAMES

My Pilgrimage

Give me my scallop-shell of quiet,
My staff of faith to walk upon,
My scrip of joy, immortal diet,
My bottle of salvation,
My gown of Glory, hope's true gage;
And thus I'll take my pilgrimage.

SIR WALTER RALEIGH

An Islamic Prayer

O God, direct me amongst those to whom Thou hast shown the right road, and keep me in safety from the calamities of this world and the next, and love me amongst those Thou hast befriended. Increase Thy favors on me, and preserve me from ill; for verily Thou canst order at Thy will, and canst not be ordered. Verily none are ruined that Thou befriendest, nor are any made great with whom Thou art at enmity.

The Lord's Prayer

After this manner therefore pray ye: Our Father which art in heaven, Hallowed be thy name.

Thy kingdom come. Thy will be done in earth, as it is in heaven.

Give us this day our daily bread.

And forgive us our debts, as we forgive our debtors.

And lead us not into temptation, but deliver us from evil: For thine is the kingdom, and the power, and the glory, for ever. Amen.

MATTHEW 6:9-13

Reason To Pray

Perhaps for saints and for truly holy men fully conscious prayer is really an everyday thing. For the ordinary worshipper, the rewards of a lifetime of faithful praying come at unpredictable times, scattered through the years, when all at once the liturgy glows as with fire. Such an hour may come after a death, or after a birth; it may flood the soul at no marked time, for no marked reason. It comes, and he knows why he has prayed all his life.

HERMAN WOUK

Homage To Thee

With Truth moving my heart,
With Best Thought inspiring my mind,
With all the might of spiritual force within me,
I kneel in homage to Thee, my Master, with
the songs of Thy loving praise ever on my lips!
And even at the last when I shall stand at Thy
Gateway as a supplicator,
I shall hear distinct the sweet echo of my
prayers from Thy Abode of Songs.

ZOROASTER

Unable To Thank Him

Though our mouths were full of song as the
sea, and our tongues of exultation as the multitude of its waves, and our lips of praise as the
wide-extended firmament; though our eyes
shone with light like the sun and the moon,
and our hands were spread forth like the eagles
of heaven, and our feet were swift as hinds, we
should still be unable to thank thee and to
bless thy name, O Lord our God and God of
our fathers, for one thousandth or one ten
thousandth part of the bounties which thou
hast bestowed upon our fathers and upon us.

THE HEBREW MORNING SERVICE

An Indian Prayer

O Thou great mystery,
Creator of the universe,
Good and powerful as Thou art,
Whose powers are displayed in
The wonders of the sun and glories of the
moon,
And the great foliage of the forest
And the great waters of the deep,
Sign of the four winds;
Whatever four corners of the earth that we
may meet—
Let us be friends, pale face and red man,
And when we come to the end of that long
trail,
And we step off into the happy hunting
ground,
From which no hunter ever returns,
Let us not only have faith in Thee—
O Thou great mystery—
But faith in each other.
O Thou Kitchin Manito, hear us!

CHIEF JOSEPH STRONGWOLF

ONE GOD FOR ALL MEN

God Loves All

All men turn their eyes to some quarter of the heavens; wherever you turn, energetically seek the good, for God will one day bring you all together.

Mohammed is no more than an apostle, and other apostles have already passed away before him. If he die, therefore, or be slain, will you turn back? Those who turn back will not weaken God at all.

If God had pleased to do so, he would surely have made you all one people. Instead, he tests you by observing your use of the talents he has given to each of you. Emulate each other, then, in good deeds, for to God you shall all return.

THE KORAN

The Over-Soul

The supreme critic of the errors of the past and the present, and the only prophet of that which must be, is that great nature in which we rest as the earth lies in the soft arms of the atmosphere, that unity, that Over-Soul, within which every man's particular being is contained and made one with all other. Within man is the soul of the whole, the wise silence, the universal beauty, to which every part and particle is equally related, the eternal One.

RALPH WALDO EMERSON

The Support of All

This is the truth: As from a blazing fire, sparks, being like unto fire, fly forth a thousandfold, thus are various beings brought forth from the Imperishable, and return thither also.

That heavenly Person is without body; He is both without and within, not produced.

From Him (when entering creation) is born breath, mind and organs of sense, ether, air, light, water and the earth, the support of all.

MUNDAKA UPANISHAD

Different Paths

You see many stars at night in the sky but find them not when the sun rises; can you say that there are no stars in the heaven of day? So, O man! because you behold not God in the days of your ignorance, say not that there is no God.

As one can ascend to the top of a house by

means of a ladder or a bamboo or a staircase or a rope, so diverse are the ways and means to approach God, and every religion in the world shows one of these ways.

Different creeds are but different paths to reach the Almighty. Various and different are the ways that lead to the temple of Mother Kali at Kalighat (Calcutta). Similarly, various are the ways that lead to the house of the Lord. Every religion is nothing but one of such paths that lead to God.

I have found that it is the same God toward whom all are directing their steps, though along different paths. You must try all beliefs and traverse all the different ways once. Wherever I look, I see men quarrelling in the name of religion—Hindus, Mohammedans, Brahmans, Vaishnavas, and the rest. But they never reflect that He who is called Krishna is also called Siva, and bears the name of the Primal Energy, Jesus and Allah as well—the same Rama with a thousand names. A lake has several ghats. At one the Hindus take water in pitchers and call it "jal"; at another the Mussalmans take water in leather bags and call it "pani." At a third the Christians call it "water." Can we imagine that it is not "jal" but only "pani" or "water"? How ridiculous! The substance is one under different names, and everyone is seeking the same substance; only climate, temperament, and name create differences. Let each man follow his own path. If he sincerely and ardently wishes to know God, peace be unto him! He will surely realize Him.

Bow down and worship where others kneel, for where so many have been paying the tribute of adoration the kind Lord must manifest Himself, for He is all mercy.

RAMAKRISHNA

Equal Respect

After long study and experience I have come to these conclusions: that (1) all religions are true, (2) all religions have some error in them, (3) all religions are almost as dear to me as my own Hinduism. My veneration for other faiths is the same as for my own faith. Consequently, the thought of conversion is impossible . . . . Our prayer for others ought never to be: "God! give them the light Thou has given to me!" but: "Give them all the light and truth they need for their highest development!"

The Allah of Islam is the same as the God of the Christian and Isvara of the Hindus. Even as there are numerous names of God in Hin-

duism, there are many names of God in Islam. The names do not indicate individuality but attributes, and little man has tried in his humble way to describe mighty God by giving Him attributes, though He is above all attributes, Indescribable, Immeasureable. Living faith in this God means equal respect for all religions. It would be the height of intolerance—and intolerance is a species of violence—to believe that your religion is superior to other religions and that you would be justified in wanting others to change over to your faith.

I believe in the fundamental truth of all great religions of the world. I believe that they are all God-given and I believe that they were necessary for the people to whom these religions were revealed. And I believe that if only we could all of us read the scriptures of the different faiths from the standpoint of the followers of these faiths, we should find that they were at the bottom all one and were all helpful to one another.

Belief in one God is the corner-stone of all religions. But I do not foresee a time when there would be only one religion on earth in practice. In theory, since there is one God, there can be only one religion. But in practice, no two persons I have known have had the same identical conception of God. Therefore, there will perhaps always be different religions answering to different temperaments and climatic conditions. MOHANDAS GANDHI

We Naturally Worship

Just as we live in different states and cities, just as we grow up with slightly different customs and speak different languages throughout the world, so do we naturally worship and believe and express our beliefs in different forms. Every thoughtful person must conclude that the most eloquent, the most magnificent conceptualizations that we can arrive at in our feeble human powers must be, in a sense, only a shallow approximation of what we feel and not a description of something that exists.

KARL MENNINGER, M.D.

The Same End

Each man must find the form of worship which suits him best, and by that I mean the form which least interferes with his habits of worship and habits of belief. Even when outward compliance is given, every man believes in God in his own way, with relative points of emphasis conditioned by his past experience. It must be so. And as long as man worships God in spirit and in truth, the forms are only means, different for different individuals, to reach the same end. LIN YUTANG

The Beatitudes

And seeing the multitudes, he went up into a mountain: and when he was set, his disciples came unto him:

And he opened his mouth, and taught them, saying,

Blessed are the poor in spirit: for theirs is the kingdom of heaven.

Blessed are they that mourn: for they shall be comforted.

Blessed are the meek: for they shall inherit the earth.

Blessed are they which do hunger and thirst after righteousness: for they shall be filled.

Blessed are the merciful: for they shall obtain mercy.

Blessed are the pure in heart: for they shall see God.

Blessed are the peacemakers: for they shall be called the children of God.

Blessed are they which are persecuted for

righteousness' sake: for theirs is the kingdom of heaven.

Blessed are ye, when men shall revile you, and persecute you, and shall say all manner of evil against you falsely, for my sake.

Rejoice, and be exceeding glad: for great is your reward in heaven: for so persecuted they the prophets which were before you.

Ye are the salt of the earth: but if the salt have lost his savour, wherewith shall it be salted? it is thenceforth good for nothing, but to be cast out, and to be trodden under foot of men.

Ye are the light of the world. A city that is set on an hill cannot be hid.

Neither do men light a candle, and put it under a bushel, but on a candlestick; and it giveth light unto all that are in the house.

Let your light so shine before men, that they may see your good works, and glorify your Father which is in heaven.

MATTHEW 5: 1-16

Universal Revelation

One must say that revelatory experiences are universally human. Religions are based on something that is given to a man wherever he lives. He is given a revelation, a particular kind of experience which always implies saving powers. One never can separate revelation and salvation. There are revealing and saving powers in all religions. God has not left himself unwitnessed. PAUL TILLICH

No Conflict

The claim that there is an inherent conflict between science and our immortal souls—that science is the natural enemy of the soul—does not stand up under examination. The man in an airplane is not necessarily less devoted to truth, justice, and charity than his forefathers in oxcarts. Virtue does not necessarily go with primitive plumbing, and human dignity can be nurtured in a skyscraper no less than in a log cabin. DAVID SARNOFF

Grace Offered

We hold that every man of good faith and right will, provided he does not sin against the light and does not refuse the grace interiorly offered to him, belongs, as we put it, to the Soul of the Church . . . and partakes of her life, which is life eternal. JACQUES MARITAIN

We who now live are parts of a humanity that extends into the remote past, a humanity that has interacted with nature. The things in civilization we most prize are not ourselves. They exist by grace of the doings and sufferings of the continuous human community in which we are a link. Ours is the responsibility of conserving, transmitting, rectifying and expanding the heritage of values we have received that those who come after us may receive it more solid and secure, more widely accessible and more generously shared than we have received it. Here are all the elements for a religious faith that shall not be confined to sect, class, or race. Such a faith has always been implicitly the common faith of mankind.

JOHN DEWEY

THE HOPE OF IMMORTALITY

Eternal Spring

Winter is on my head but eternal spring is in my heart. The nearer I approach the end, the plainer I hear around me the immortal symphonies of the world to come. For half a century I have been writing my thoughts in prose and verse; but I feel that I have not said one-thousandth part of what is in me. When I have gone down to the grave I shall have ended my day's work; but another day will begin the next morning. Life closes in the twilight but opens with the dawn.   VICTOR HUGO

Heaven and Earth

The way of Heaven and earth may be completely declared in one sentence: They are without any doubleness, and so they produce things in a manner that is unfathomable.

The way of Heaven and earth is large and substantial, high and brilliant, far-reaching and long-continuing.

All things are nourished together without their injuring one another. The courses of the seasons, and of the sun and moon are pursued without any collision among them. The smaller energies are like river-currents; the greater energies are seen in mighty transformations. It is this which makes Heaven and earth so great.

He who is greatly virtuous will be sure to receive the appointment of Heaven.

CONFUCIUS

> From the unreal lead me to the real.
> From darkness lead me to light.
> From death lead me to immortality.

THE UPANISHADS

A Force That Cannot Die

There are two men in each one of us: the scientist, he who starts with clear field and desires to rise to the knowledge of Nature through observation, experimentation and reasoning; and the man of sentiment, the man of faith, the man who mourns his dead children and who cannot, alas, prove at all that he will see them again, but who believes that he will, and lives in that hope . . . . The man who feels that force that is within him cannot die.

LOUIS PASTEUR

One Author

All mankind is of one author and is one volume; when one man dies, one chapter is not torn out of the book, but translated into a better language; and every chapter must be so translated . . . . God's hand is in every translation.   JOHN DONNE

Celestial Glory

We are made for the splendor of celestial glory. If the Lord also reserves for us a little honor on earth, this is of no value at all and perishes quickly if it is not of God. If the Lord, on the contrary, disposes that the value of our life be entirely hidden in Him, it would be ridiculous to look for anything else. The ambitious are the most ridiculous and the most pitiful creatures on the earth.   POPE JOHN XXIII

Eternal Existence

When I see nothing annihilated and not even a drop of water wasted, I cannot suspect the annihilation of souls, or believe that He will suffer the daily waste of millions of minds ready made that now exist and put Himself to the continual trouble of making new ones. Thus finding myself to exist in the world, I believe I shall, in some shape or other, always exist; and, with all the inconveniences human life is liable to, I shall not object to a new edition of mine; hoping, however, that the errata of the last may be corrected.

BENJAMIN FRANKLIN

Only a Guess

Science cannot supply a definite answer to the question of immortality. Immortality relates to an aspect of life which is not physical, that is, which cannot be detected and measured by any instrument, and to which the application of the laws of science can at best be only a well-considered guess.

ARTHUR H. COMPTON

Man Will Prevail

I decline to accept the end of man. It is easy enough to say that man is immortal simply because he will endure; that when the last dingdong of doom has clanged and faded from the last worthless rock hanging tideless in the last red and dying evening, that even then there

will still be one more sound: that of his puny inexhaustible voice, still talking. I refuse to accept this. I believe that man will not merely endure: he will prevail. He is immortal, not because he alone among creatures has an inexhaustible voice, but because he has a soul, a spirit capable of compassion and sacrifice and endurance.   WILLIAM FAULKNER

Immortal Longings

I believe in the immortality of the soul because I have within me immortal longings. I believe that the state we enter after death is wrought of our own motives, thoughts and deeds. I believe that in the life to come I shall have the senses I have not had here, and that my home there will be beautiful with colour, music, the speech of flowers and faces I love.

HELEN KELLER

Unsurpassable Vision

When I go from hence let this be my parting word, that what I have seen is unsurpassable.

I have tasted of the hidden honey of this lotus that expands on the ocean of light, and thus am I blessed—let this be my parting word.

In this playhouse of infinite forms I have had my play and here have I caught sight of him that is formless.

My whole body and my limbs have thrilled with his touch who is beyond touch; and if the end comes here, let it come—let this be my parting word.   RABINDRANATH TAGORE

The Soul of Man

If the Father deigns to touch with divine power the cold and pulseless heart of the buried acorn and to make it burst forth from its prison walls, will He leave neglected in the earth the soul of man made in the image of his Creator?

WILLIAM JENNINGS BRYAN

A New Infinite

It is the great mystery of human life that old grief passes gradually into quiet, tender joy. The mild serenity of age takes the place of the riotous blood of youth. I bless the rising sun each day, and, as before, my heart sings to meet it, but now I love even more its setting, its long slanting rays and the soft, tender, gentle memories that come with them, the dear images from the whole of my long, happy life—and over all the Divine Truth, softening, reconciling, forgiving!

My life is ending, I know that well, but every day that is left me I feel how my earthly life is in touch with a new infinite, unknown, but approaching life, the nearness of which sets my soul quivering with rapture, my mind glowing and my heart weeping with joy.

FYODOR DOSTOEVSKI

Fear not that thy life shall come to an end, but rather fear that it shall never have a beginning.

CARDINAL NEWMAN

Set in Trump Mediæval, a Venetian face designed by
Professor Georg Trump of Munich, Germany.
Typography by Grant Dahlstrom,
set at The Castle Press.
Printed on Hallmark Eggshell Book paper.
Designed by Virginia Orchard.